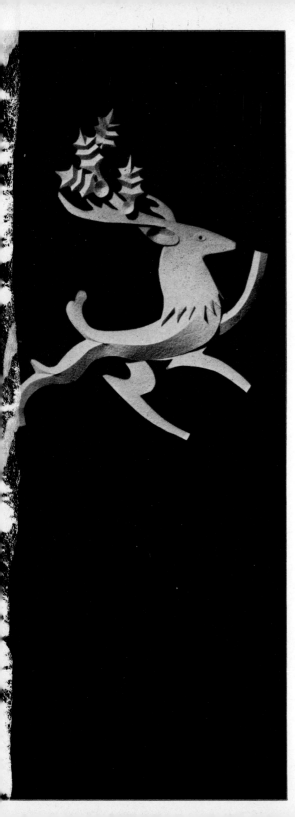

An Introduction to
PAPER SCULPTURE

The author with two of his designs

ARTHUR SADLER
F.R.S.A.

An Introduction to
PAPER
SCULPTURE

LONDON
BLANDFORD PRESS

First Published 1965
Second Impression 1971
© Blandford Press Ltd, 1965
167 High Holborn, London WC1V 6PH

ISBN 0 7137 0388 1

ACKNOWLEDGMENTS
I wish to thank Tunbridge Studios, London, for collaboration and interest
in the photography of the finished examples of my sculptures for this book.
Also Campbell Press Studios, London, for the photography of many
of the making details of the sculptures.
My sincere thanks to Robert Forrester for his assistance
and interest in the preparation of this book.
Arthur Sadler.

Printed in Great Britain by
Tonbridge Printers Ltd, Peach Hall Works, Tonbridge, Kent.

Contents

6 Designs 20

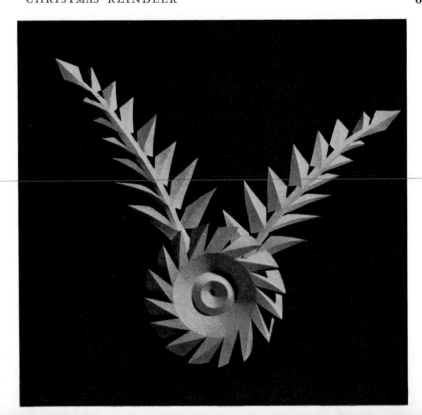

Foreword

GREAT PLEASURE CAN BE DERIVED from Paper Sculpture as an artistic and interesting hobby which offers great scope for self-expression. Expense does not enter into it as the materials required can be obtained very cheaply. Variation in design is dependent wholly upon the ingenuity of the artist. Other aspects in its favour are its lightness in weight and it can therefore be fixed easily in any desired position. It is also very durable and clean to handle which makes it a suitable hobby for the home. There are many uses for paper sculpture as a form of decoration in the home, schools, exhibitions, advertisement layouts and photography. The value, therefore, of this medium for a student planning a career in design and decoration is obvious.

I was first impressed with paper sculpture from examples seen as decorations on the Continent and, as a result of its fascinating appearance, experimented in the production of small pieces as a hobby. Patience and experience gained resulted in creations which were used to good effect in window displays and exhibitions. Later, requests were made for me to teach the craft to others and I wrote the first book on Paper Sculpture to be published in England.

This book describes the technique of building various kinds of paper sculpture and shows many examples of it. The reader will realise that it is often easier to demonstrate the creation of a given piece of work than it is to describe it in words; forbearance is therefore sought if the seemingly simplest details have been emphasised in an effort to provide clarity and understanding of the technique required.

If the exercises on the manipulation of paper are mastered first the beginner can soon move on to make actual decorations. The pieces given in this book are intended for the beginner to study and to see quickly the possibilities of this art form but need not be slavishly copied. One's own ideas of interpretation of the subject will then emerge which is the whole purpose of this book and will, I hope, encourage many to create worth-while and satisfying paper sculptures.

Brighton,   ARTHUR SADLER, F.R.S.A.
Sussex.

Paper Sculpture

OCCASIONALLY IN THE HISTORY of the graphic arts, artistic experiment evolves a really new technique. In the course of time this may develop into a new art form. From the centuries-old methods of peasant paper craft, Paper Sculpture as we see it today has followed that course. This firmly established and expressive medium is an art form in its own right. In fact, based as it is on the building up in relief from sheet materials, it differs greatly in primary concept and manipulative technique from all familiar media, as you will see from the examples given on the following pages.

8

1 The Principles of Paper Sculpture

PAPER SCULPTURE IS SO CALLED from its final appearance rather than being true sculpture. The word SCULPTURE is derived from a root meaning "to cut" as one might cut in stone. While Paper Sculpture is formed as much by scoring, folding and bending as it is by cutting, the term is still not inexact. All sculpture involves the shaping of a surface so that the appearance of form emerges. The limitations of the paper itself involves modifications of form from the actual subject. Without modification the sculpture would not catch the light and thus convey the proper appearance of form. The sculptor of paper must coax his material into the appearance of the form he wishes to represent and portray simplified and flattened planes in convincing solidity. If you compare a paper sculpture with a flat picture the sharp edges take the place of the lines of the composition. The soft ones give it body by the effect of light and shade.

Paper Sculpture is composed of flat sheets of paper rolled, bent, scored, cut and folded to produce a three-dimensional form. The sheet of paper is flat and two dimensional. It can be rolled into a tube and as it is bent it gains in strength and at the same time its roundness gives the appearance of solidity. In fact Paper Sculpture just capitalises on these created effects and shows that bent paper is stronger than in the flat sheet. It becomes a mere shell giving the illusion of volume, and the appearance of solid sculpture.

It will be understood by now the vital part the manipulation of the paper plays. By doing the elementary exercises on the following pages, the beginner learns the limitations and possibilities in manipulating paper to express ideas and create designs in Paper Sculpture which have as much art quality as those done in other materials.

9

2 Tools and Materials

THE BASIC TOOLS required for the craft of paper sculpture are quite simple and most of them can be found in the majority of homes. Illustrated are all the tools used for the work in this book.

THE PAPER

You will need a good quality paper which is pliable but will not tear or crumple. Beginners should experiment with a good cartridge paper and, as they become accustomed to manipulating paper without waste, should then move on to using drawing papers of the hand-made variety in rough or smooth finish depending upon the effect desired. Work at first in white paper in order to appreciate the effect of light and shade on the pieces created. Later, if colour is desired, use poster paints to colour the paper.

THE TOOLS

Scissors are required—a pair with long blades, a pair with shorter blades and more pointed—and also a pair of curved nail scissors if possible. Knives can be of any kind with a short blade. A stencil knife is the most useful for scoring paper. A wooden knife is useful for folding paper. There is a tool called a Swann Morton Craft Tool. This has two blades fitted into a handle and ideal for cutting paper and cardboard. This kind of tool is not essential but most useful. Rulers, one of wood and one of metal, are essential. Compasses, set-square, pencils, rubber, pins and paper fasteners are necessary. A staple gun of the office type is most useful to join two or three pieces of paper together and also to fasten paper to a background of cardboard if required. It must be hinged so that the stapling surface will operate lying flat.

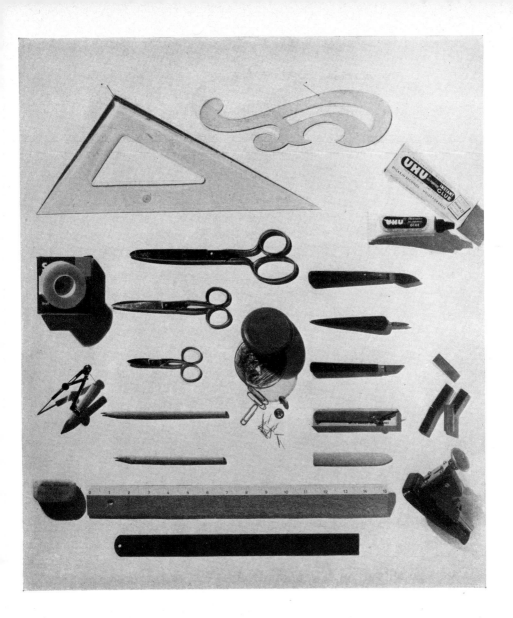

ADHESIVES

Any glues which are strong, dry quickly and are clear are suitable. All my work is done with UHU—an instant glue—obtainable from most stationers and Woolworths. Gum tape, too, is required.

3 Cutting Paper and Cardboard

Cutting and scoring are the only two technical processes to paper sculpture. Both require a delicate touch and a direct approach.

Knives of any description can be used for cutting paper. A pad of old cardboard or paper between the bench and the object being cut is essential. This not only protects the bench top but gives the work a bed that keeps it from slipping. To cut a straight line use a metal rule or guide which should be held firmly with the left hand. The right hand holding the knife should be more relaxed than the left. If the knife is sharp it will require little pressure to cut through the paper. Beginners will be well advised to have pencil lines to follow for both cutting and scoring. Eye and hand co-ordinate in following a pencilled line.

To follow a curved or wavy line the paper is moved by the left hand to follow the shape either round or back and forth while the knife is held in place by the right hand. This ensures an even flowing cut. All shapes should be cut out with a knife rather than scissors. When the beginner becomes used to it a knife gives a cleaner cut. The artist in paper sculpture will eventually find his favourite cutting tool which may be a knife, blunt razor blade or a stencil knife. The last is a very useful tool for young students or beginners. To cut cardboard with a knife do not try to press hard and cut in one stroke. Cut several even strokes following the same line carefully until the cardboard is separated from end to end. The start and end always require an extra stroke or so depending upon whether you are an enthusiastic starter or finisher.

4 Basic Shaping

Paper may be shaped in two basic ways to give an effect of roundness and solidity—either by bending or folding. For full roundness it can be bent into tubes or cones, and for low relief effects bent only part way round forming a bow or arc.

When paper is folded to give a sharp transition from one plane to another an angular break made by scoring can be used.

On the following pages the important part the scoring and folding plays in the making of paper sculpture is clearly demonstrated.

SCORING PAPER

Scoring is one of the most used methods in folding paper. The process means that the paper surface is cut halfway through so that the paper will bend away from the cut surface. To score bear very lightly on the knife blade. If the scoring is made too deeply the paper will break away when folded. In scoring straight lines a metal ruler should be used. The exact amount of pressure should be determined by making trial cuts on the type of paper used for each item.

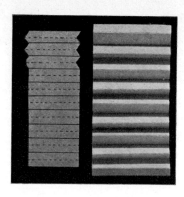

SHADOW FOLDS

As dark and light play an important part in paper sculpture so do the folds that are responsible for the contrasts. Take a sheet of drawing paper and with a pencil and ruler draw lines one inch apart on one side of the paper. With a knife score these lines. Turn the paper over and draw dotted lines between the lines already scored on the reverse side of the paper. Score these dotted lines. Holding the paper, fold back and forth into a series of reverse folds. The fold is one of the commonest devices used in paper sculpture. The sharp turn breaks up the surface into a pattern of light and dark. Note too that folding paper stiffens it, giving it more strength.

A FIVE-POINTED STAR

Draw a five-pointed star as shown and cut out. On one side pencil lines from each point to their common meeting place at the centre. Score these lines. Turn the star over and draw dotted lines from the centre to the crotches and score. Using both hands fold the long scores up and fold the short scores down using the knife blade to get the folds sharp at the centre. You can see from this exercise how form emerges from a flat sheet of paper, also that paper can be folded by the way it is scored on either side of the paper.

CONCENTRIC CIRCLE DESIGN

One of the most satisfying designs and yet simple to construct is a design of concentric circles. On a sheet of paper draw a circle and cut it out. On this circle draw three inner circles, two on one side (indicated by lines in the diagram) and on the reverse side by the dotted line. Score these lines and cut out a segment of paper from the circle.

Bend the scoring on both sides, mould into a circle and secure by overlapping the edges which should be glued. Many variations of design are possible, governed by the number of the circles.

SCORED CURVES

Curves are beautiful structures but, unlike straight lines, they cannot be creased without first being scored with a knife or other instrument. Shown here are a few curves which may be drawn free hand. Beginners should experiment with making a single curve at first, then reverse curves. Paper scored with a curved line no longer remains flat but becomes three-dimensional. When two lines are scored one bends in the opposite direction from the other. Every other line is bent upwards and alternate lines go down. The application of scored curves will be found throughout this book.

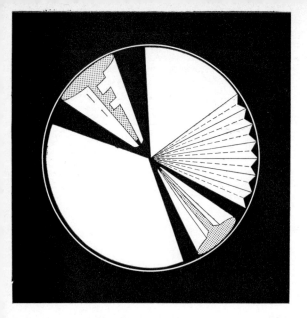

CYLINDERS AND TUBES

Paper curved into tubes or cylinders should first be made pliable. To do this draw a sheet of paper under the steel rule held firmly down on the bench. Repeat on both sides of the paper until supple. The cylinder in all sizes is the foundation of paper sculpture in the round. To make a cylinder simply roll a sheet of paper and fasten the edges firmly with glue. Stand on a flat surface and it will support anything you wish to attach to it. Note how the bending strengthens the paper.

CONES

Cones can be used in many ways in paper sculpture and are made from segments of a circle (see diagram). If the cone is to be slender, use a narrow segment of the circular shape cutting from the centre to the circumference in a straight line. To make wider cones use almost the complete circle. The radius of the circle decides the height of the cone.

A FEW BASIC SHAPES

Cones can be fastened with glue attached to the overlapping edges or tabs can be used which must be added in the making. These are afterwards locked into slits on the paper cone with glue (see diagram). Cones can be pleated. Use a whole circle of paper and score lines alternatively on each side of the paper. Cut through to the centre of the circle and pleat into shape. A section of such a cone can be seen in the diagram.

CURLING PAPER FOR DECORATIVE EFFECTS

Pieces of paper can be curled for decorative effects by using the scissor blades. Take a strip of paper, hold with one hand and place the paper over the scissor blade. With the thumb on top draw the thumb and scissor blade down the paper and a curl will be effected. This method is used to curl hair styles, flower petals, leaves, etc.

CUT SURFACE TREATMENT

The surface of a flat sheet of paper can be transformed into a pattern of light and shadow and is also given texture by cutting into the surface of the paper at intervals with a knife. Designs formed like this are not only interesting backgrounds in themselves but are useful for surface treatment of the paper to indicate fish scales, feathers, leaves, etc. This will be seen in many of the sculptures in this book.

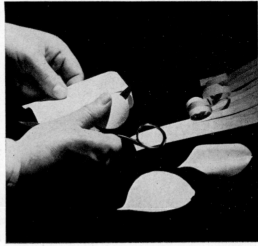

PART TWO

COMPLETED SCULPTURES TO MAKE

5 Construction

SO FAR YOU HAVE LEARNED how to handle the paper for the making of Paper Sculpture. Now we come to the actual construction of many pieces. Some paper sculptures are designed to be mounted upon a background panel. Other low relief paper sculptures are supported on a cardboard or other foundation cut to the outline of the main form. Successive layers of paper are curved over this foundation and secured at the back with tabs of paper and glue. The paper for such sculptures is cut wider than the foundation to allow for belling out as you turn it over the foundation. This gives it a solid effect.

Full relief sculpture to be seen from all sides requires a little more experience to produce a good result. Several examples are illustrated. Figures require an armature or other support unless they are just small cone constructions which would therefore stand alone. Other sculptures such as birds in full relief need a support in order to make them stand and be seen from all sides. It is always advisable to make preliminary sketches to show the proportions. Anyone interested in constructing models soon develops the skill in assembling the various parts to make a sculptured design.

The designs for finished paper sculptures which follow in the next chapter are made by using all the methods of manipulating paper in the exercises already carried out. If you study and make these completed sculptures you will gain an overall knowledge of the craft. You need not follow them slavishly but may just use them for inspiration. As you proceed many ideas for constructing your own designs will emerge which is the real purpose of this book. As in painting and drawing, there is no end to the methods of expression and it remains for the artist in paper sculpture to explore and expand this art form.

HORSE'S HEAD DESIGN

6 Designs

HORSE'S HEAD DESIGN IN RELIEF PAPER SCULPTURE

If you have experimented with the handling of paper to the instructions given on the previous pages, you will now be familiar with the working principles of paper sculpture and ready to go on to the making of a real piece of decoration.

THE HORSE'S HEAD

This is to be made in low relief and fixed to a background panel when completed. The first stage is to draw and cut out in stout paper the horse's head (1). Next with a fine pencil draw in the lines where indicated and also pencil in the shape of the eye and nostril (2–3). Now score and crease the black lines on the head. Make a small cut each side of the base of the ear (4) and crease the centre line into shape. Next cut through the half circle lines made for the eye and nostril (2–3). Lift the eye and sink the nostril. This should by now have changed what was a flat cut-out shape into a moulded head. The mane comes next. Draw and cut out pattern (5) for the upper part of the mane. Score and crease where indicated. Next draw, cut out and score and crease the pattern (6) for the lower part of the mane. The three pieces of sculpture are now ready to assemble into a complete head. Position the mane (5) behind the head piece and fasten with pieces of gum tape to the back of the head. Next the lower part of the mane (6) is fixed in the same way with a strip of gum tape. The complete head should now be loosely held together. Next bend back the paper tabs and put spots of glue on them and also on the spots (X) on the back of the head. The head can now be fixed in position upon the panel background.

DECORATIVE SCROLLS AND ORNAMENTS

This kind of classical design has a great appeal in paper, bringing out a true sculptural effect.

Historical and architectural books should be studied for innumerable decorative or ornamental forms suitable to interpret into paper sculpture. The Baroque period is very interesting. Shapes can be used alone on panels, in groups, or continuously as borders and for frames. Each design is most effective if it is kept simple and conventional in character. French curves can be used in order to simplify the drawing and designing of such ornaments. Scrolls can be attached to a background by fastening a strip of paper to the back of them with gum tape. To mount, cut a slash in the background and force the two ends of the strip of paper through, fixing them at the back with more gum tape. Beginners will enjoy making scroll designs for it needs little practice to turn out a satisfactory piece of work.

A SCULPTURED FRAME

This frame is constructed over a flat frame of cardboard, 21 in. square and 3 in. wide. This is covered with the same paper you are to use to make the sixteen paper sculptured scrolls which decorate it.

MAKING THE SCROLLS

Draw the two patterns for the scrolls as indicated. They are 5 in. long. Note that they are in reverse—making a pair. Pencil in the lines indicated for the scoring—the plain lines on one side of the paper and the dotted lines on the reverse. Cut out the scrolls and score the plain and dotted lines. Mould into shape. You have now completed two scrolls but will require sixteen—eight of each design. Use the two scrolls you have as templates and draw round them to make eight of each design. These are then cut out and scored and folded as already instructed. To complete, the scrolls are mounted in pairs as shown on the completed frame. Secure the scrolls to the frame with spots of glue placed on the back of them.

MAKING A FLEUR-DE-LIS IN RELIEF PAPER CUTTING

This classic design should be drawn on a sheet of paper indicating where the scoring is to be on the top side (the fine lines). Score these with the knife. Cut out the design and on the reverse side indicate the scoring by the dotted lines. Score these.

Now mould into shape, getting a good centre crease and nice curves at the sides.

The centre band is made from a circle of paper with concentric

circles drawn on to it. These circles should be scored, the ones indicated by the line on one side of the paper and by the dotted line on the reverse side. Cut a piece out of the circle and mould into shape. Try the centre band around the decoration and, where it fits over the centre crease, cut out a V piece in order to fit neatly into place. Fasten the centre band behind the decoration with gum tape.

The Fleur-de-Lis design is now complete. This piece of sculpture in all white would be most effective mounted upon a blue background.

LEAF DESIGN SCULPTURED OVAL FRAME

This superb frame is quite easy to construct. It is made by using an oval cardboard foundation. The moulded pieces in the form of paper leaves are stapled in place on this foundation.

MAKING THE LEAF DESIGN PAPER SCULPTURE

Draw a pattern as shown using compasses and a ruler (note the circles have only been left in as a guide to drawing the pattern). Cut out the pattern and next cut down the centre lines to the circle centres. Turn the paper over and score down the centre line indicated by the dotted line, using the metal ruler as a guide.

Next cross the two cut strips, 1 and 2, pulling the circle pieces round into a cone shape in doing so. This brings the design into relief. Stick the strips together where they cross but not to the back piece. Cut

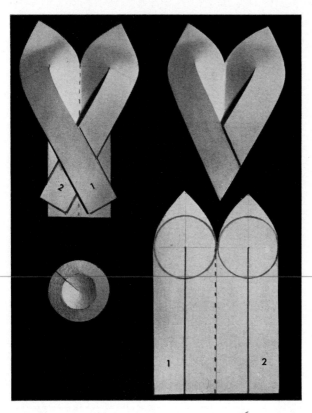

off the surplus paper as shown. This completes the leaf design sculpture.

You will need a few of these leaf sculptures to complete a frame, so make a template of the pattern outline—you can draw round this—and cut out a few leaves at a time including the centre line cuts. All you have to do then is to score the dotted line on the back of each, mould into shape and stick with glue.

When you have completed a quantity they are then assembled on to the oval frame foundation by overlapping and stapling to the frame as you proceed.

The frame is finished by two circles of paper—cut through to the centre scored as shown and glued overlapping the edges. They are then glued to the decoration where the reversed garlands of leaves meet, top and bottom.

FLOWERS AND LEAVES

When making paper sculptured flowers and leaves do not try to make an exact replica but keep the design as simple as possible. It is advisable to interpret nature in a free style and at the same time satisfy a creative impulse. By using the effects of light and shade on a simple stylised flower a very good impression of the natural flower will emerge. The fundamental basis for most stylised sculptured flowers is a circular cut-out made into a cone which can be deep or shallow and from which the petal shapes are cut. Below and on the following pages are a few flower designs to illustrate how attractive stylised flower designs can be.

STYLISED DAFFODILS

Draw and cut out the flower shape as shown in the diagram. Score the black lines on one side and where the dotted lines indicate on the reverse side. Cut a circle out of the centre and bend the scoring on both sides of the flower shape. Next make a small cone and place through the hole in the flower shape for a trumpet. This is to be kept in position with a circle of gum tape placed over the cone where it protrudes at the back of the flower. Place a wire with a tiny circle of

paper fixed to it through the centre of the cone for a stem. Finish by wrapping the wire with thin paper. These flowers can be mounted on a panel in groups with a few simple leaves cut from paper with a scored centre vein. They could also be arranged in a vase design made from paper.

CALA LILY DESIGN

THE CALA LILY

The cala lily pattern is cut from a triangular piece of paper. Draw the outline as shown curving two sides and leaving one side straight. Along the straight side draw a tab piece as shown and next cut out the whole shape. Now draw a continuous curve around the two sides. Score and bend. The lily should be moulded into a cone-like shape and, in doing so, note where the tab piece would join the longer side of the lily. Mark this position and cut a slit in the paper. Through this slit the tab of paper is passed and fixed with a little glue holding it in position until the glue sets.

The stamen is made from a strip of paper curled by rolling it around a pencil. It is fastened through the centre of the lily with a little glue. The stems are cut from a double thickness of paper in straight or curved lines. The leaves, too, are cut to shape, scored and folded. These lilies were designed to be fixed to a panel with pins or glue.

Note the assembly of these blooms on the completed panel. They have a classic sculptural quality.

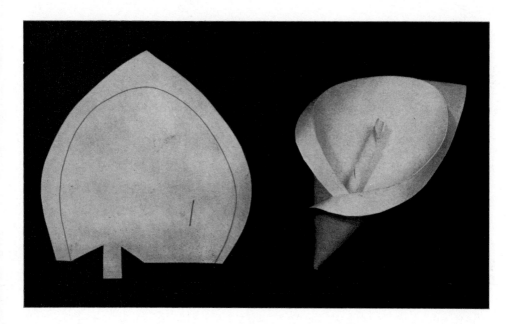

DECORATIVE LEAF DESIGNS

DECORATIVE LEAVES

The beginner should collect real leaves and study them noting the great variety of shapes nature provides. These leaves can be pressed and kept for future reference. Leaves make an interesting arrangement on a panel using several different shapes together. They may also be used for border designs and to supplement other items to make a decoration. Bouquets and flower arrangements need the addition of leaves to complete the ensemble. Leaves make classical garlands which are most effective in paper sculpture. The following paragraphs give details of how to make different types of leaves.

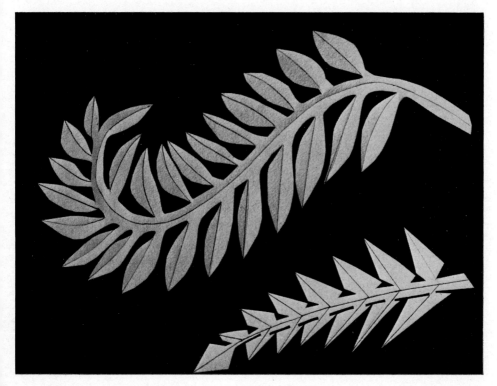

THE HOLLY LEAF

Draw the leaf on a piece of paper as shown below. Mark the veins on both sides of the paper with a pencil, using plain lines on the top side and dotted lines on the reverse. Score the lines on both sides of the leaf. With both hands mould the plain lines down and the dotted lines up. This is a little more difficult than folding straight lines but a little practice will enable you to master this type of folding. The leaf below the holly leaf in the illustration is made in the same manner.

THE CURVED LEAF

This type of leaf needs to be made large to be effective. As a guide this one was cut from a piece of paper 18 in. long by 12 in. wide. The design of this leaf is governed by the curve of the centre stem so that is drawn first.

The leaf formations on each side of the stem must be drawn separately but the centre vein of each must connect with the centre stem. The leaf is now cut out and scored and folded to create a pattern of light and shade.

STYLISED LEAF

This interesting design is again made up from a centre stem from which the vein formation governing the reverse folded spiky leaves emanates. Note the slot-like cuts on the left-hand side of the leaf—changing the design of that side of the leaf. After cutting out and scoring the leaf is folded. In this design the veins join into the centre vein. All these leaves are designed to be used mounted upon a background. If they are to be used for an arrangement to stand alone they would need to be supported down the centre vein or stem. This can be done by fixing covered flower wire with glue to the back of the leaf, of course following the shape of the leaf stem and leaving sufficient wire to arrange in your design. For some schemes thin cardboard can be used instead of the wire for this support.

ENGLISH ROSE DESIGN

ENGLISH ROSE DESIGN

Here is a beautiful flower design—the rose. To make it draw and cut out a spiral of paper as shown in the pattern. This should next be rolled with a ruler to make the paper more pliable in the hand for the purpose of moulding into shape. After this treatment the paper spiral is rolled by hand into a rose shape. Start from the flat end of the spiral but do not roll too far at first. Bring the rest of the spiral round loosely and then insert the rounded end into the spiral. You can manipulate the rose shape until you are satisfied with its design, open wide or closed. It can then be glued or stapled together.

These roses were made to assemble in an interesting grouping upon a background. They were pinned in place and spots of glue used where needed. The leaves are made by folding a piece of paper after it has been scored and then cutting out the leaf shape. The edges of the leaf can be curled with the scissor blade or knife for effect. The leaves, too, were arranged in the bouquet design with a spot of glue as were also the spots of paper to complete the design.

AFRICAN MASK

MASKS FOR DECORATION

Throughout the ages man has used the face as a source of design, the Greeks notably in the masks of Humour and Drama and the classical masks depicting the Gods. Peoples of other lands, Japanese, Chinese, Mexicans, Aztecs and African tribes produced masks from all kinds of materials. Carved wood native masks, even the very primitive ones, are often very spirited and show a great simplification of line. The work from all these sources is well worth studying. Books on stage design and the theatre which show these decorative masks can be borrowed from libraries.

There are subtleties to be considered because of the exaggeration of shape and line, so it is possible for one with little experience to design a very satisfactory composition.

Paper sculptured masks make interesting panel designs along with flower garlands, classical scrolls or drapes, all done in the same medium paper.

Paper sculptured masks were designed by the artist Picasso for the first cubist ballet "Parade" in 1937. It is not difficult to design masks to be worn at festivals or on the stage.

MAKING THE MASK ILLUSTRATED

The African mask illustrated opposite, as you can see, relies upon its decorative shape for much of its attraction. It is given depth simply by the scored centre line to the design. Here is a clear example of the effect of light and shade achieved by planes.

CLASSIC MASK

Start by drawing the oval face shape (1) on a sheet of heavy paper. Outline with a pencil the eyes, mouth and ears. Cut out the eyes and mouth with a sharp knife. Next cut slits down the side of the ears (X). The pieces at the side of the head need to be large enough to be carried round to the back in order to make the head stand away from the background in relief.

Next the forehead construction is drawn (2). Pencil in the lines indicating the forehead and nose. This shape is to create a shadow around the eye. Score these lines (X) and press back forming the nose. This piece of sculpture (2) is placed over the face shape (1). Bend back the side lines indicated. These go into the ear slits until the piece is level with the top edge of the mask. Next cut a slit in the face to take the tab of the nose piece which is bent back into the slit and secured with glue. Next the shape for the cheeks is drawn on paper (3) and cut out. Pencil and score the lines (O) and bend into shape. Cut slits where indicated (X). Bend these round behind the cheek and secure with glue.

This decorative mask is completed by fixing to a panel and adding leaves of a type you have already been instructed to make.

CLASSIC MASK DESIGN

41

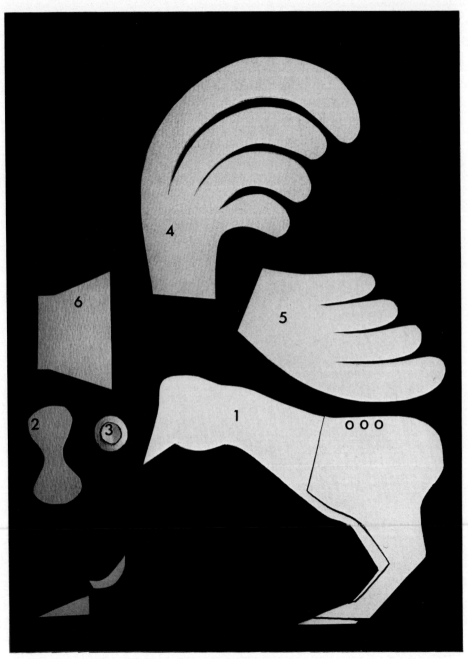

COCKERELS

These birds are made upon a cardboard construction enabling them to stand alone. They are in full relief paper sculpture. First a sheet of cardboard is covered both sides with the paper you are to use. This completed, draw the body construction (1) and cut out. Next the rear portion only is duplicated and by glueing this at the top only (O), the construction will open out to stand. The comb and wattles are next cut out in paper only (2). Cut the edges top and bottom and glue in place on the head. Next the eye. This is a scored circle. Make and glue where indicated on the finished bird.

The tall tail feathers come next (4). Draw and cut out in paper and score the feathers with a centre crease on the surface only and fold. Fix to the construction with glue. Make the wing feathers in the same manner from shape (5) and fix in position on the body. The feather piece (6) is cut to shape, slashed at the edge and curled a little then glued over the wing feathers where indicated. Complete the bird with claws and spurs fixed to the feet and legs after the bird has been glued by the legs to a base of cardboard. For the bird to be seen all round it is obvious the details will need to be made in duplicate and fixed to each side of the body construction.

MERMAID DESIGN

44

A MERMAID

Here is a delightful little figure in low relief sculpture which will stand alone. First cover a piece of cardboard with the type of paper you are to use for this work. This is to form the foundation of the mermaid and rock. Next draw shape (1) on this foundation and cut out.

Now to make the paper relief sculpture to cover this foundation. First draw the face shape (2) and cut it out. This is fixed in place over the cardboard construction by the top tab over the head and the neck is fixed to the body. Next the tail shape (3) is drawn and a pencil line indicates the curved line to be scored and folded. The scales are cut with the knife and raised. This piece is not positioned to the lower part of the mermaid. Fasten the tabs with glue bending them behind the construction. Next draw, cut out and score where indicated shape (4). Fix this with a spot of glue under the tail to the base of the model (X). Next draw tail shape (5). Cut out, score and fold and fix behind the other tail piece where shown. Glue in position. Draw the hair shapes (6) and (7). Cut out and curl as instructed previously and fix (7) behind the head and (6) to the front of the head. Next the arm (8) is cut out and bent behind the head after glueing to the elbow. Complete by simple details for face features. Add the starfish to the base. This figure will stand alone if a strut is glued behind it.

FISHES AND MARINE LIFE FOR DECORATION

Fishes and under sea plant life make interesting subjects for decorative designs as you will see from a study of the panel illustrated.

MAKING THE SMALL FISHES AND THE SEA HORSE

The small round fish shown at the top of the patterns is made from a sheet of paper with the fish drawn upon it and cut out to shape. Cut out the eye, pencil in the black lines and score them. Mould the scoring and in doing so you will notice how the simple fold brings out the form desired.

The triangular shaped fish is drawn and cut out, the black lines pencilled in, scored and folded. The scales on this fish are made by the cut surface treatment—cut through with the knife and raised. This creates a pattern of light and shade.

The sea horse is drawn and cut to shape, scored down the spine after the line indicated has been pencilled in, then moulded into shape. The fins are drawn and cut out to the shape shown, the lines indicating the scoring pencilled in, black lines on one side and dotted lines on the reverse. Score and mould into folds. The fins are then fixed into position behind the body with glue or gum tape.

The seaweed plant. This is just a curved cut out piece of paper, scored with a curved line and folded into shape—simple yet very effective.

MARINE LIFE PANEL

47

DECORATIVE FISH DESIGN

This fish design is to be made in half relief paper sculpture. First a cardboard foundation is made of the outline of the body of the fish. This is not shown but has to be made as the body shape (1) and should be cut a little smaller. This is to allow the paper body to be bent in an arc around the cardboard foundation, belling out the paper by fastening behind the foundation with the glued paper tabs.

MAKING THE BODY

Draw and cut out in paper the body covering pattern (1). Draw in the lines to indicate the scoring and then score. Make fine pencil lines to indicate the scales. These are given a cut surface treatment by cutting them through with the knife and raising them up from the surface. Next bend into shape the scored lines. This paper sculptured body is now ready to be fixed over the cardboard body as described above.

THE TAIL

This is drawn to shape, the lines indicating the scoring pencilled in, plain lines on one side and dotted lines on the reverse. Score and fold the tail into shape. The tail is now positioned behind the body of the fish and secured with glue or gum tape.

THE FINS

Draw, cut out and score the detail where indicated on the three fins. The fins are then fixed as follows. The fin on the back of the fish is fixed behind the body with glue or gum tape. The small fin under the fish is fixed in the same manner. The curved fin is placed in a slit cut into the body of the fish having had glue put on the end of it before doing so.

THE EYE

This is a circle cut to the centre with a circle scored on to it. Pull round and glue overlapping the edges. The eye can now be fixed in position with a spot of glue.

This now completes an interesting piece of paper sculpture ready to be mounted upon a background or panel.

Many types of fish can be made in this manner for decoration. Angel fish with sweeping tails look most effective. Shells, too, can be fashioned by rolling paper shapes. All these make good subjects for design.

CHRISTMAS ANGEL

This tall figure in full relief sculpture is constructed over an armature
as follows. The armature was made from a poster cylinder, 22 in.
high. This was cut into 2 in. strips at the base. The strips were bent
back and glued to a cardboard base. This made the armature 20 in.
high which is the height of the completed figure. Four inches down
from the top of the tube a dowel of wood 4 in. long was pushed cross-
ways through holes in the tube. This supports the arms and is used to
build the shoulder details.

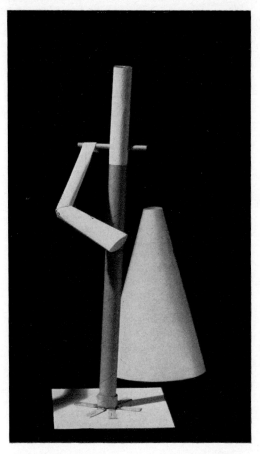

ARMATURE CONSTRUCTION
FOR CHRISTMAS ANGEL

For the actual paper sculpture make a cone of paper $11\frac{1}{2}$ in. tall by 6 in. in diameter at the base. This is for the skirt construction which is placed over the armature, removing the dowel in order to do so. Fix to the tube and before replacing the dowel cover the top part of the tube with paper.

Shape (2). The sleeves come next and they are made from cones of paper $10\frac{3}{4}$ in. long with a diamond cut out to indicate the elbow bends. Fix these to the dowels as shown in the armature construction.

The upper part of the dress is made next. Cut out shape (3) which is 15 in. long and $4\frac{3}{4}$ in. at the widest part. Cut a hole in this $1\frac{1}{2}$ in. in diameter and place over the tube and dowel and fix at the front and back of the figure with glue.

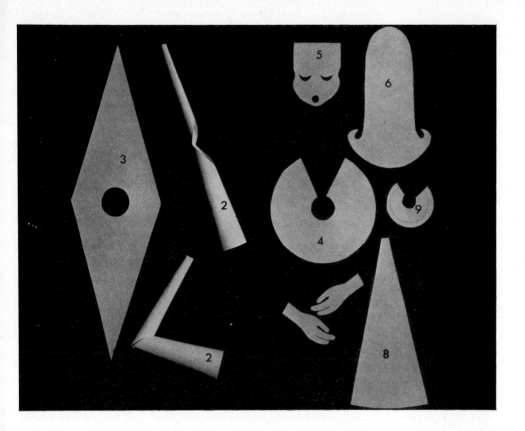

The collar shape (4) is a circle of paper $5\frac{1}{2}$ in. in diameter with a hole in the centre $1\frac{1}{2}$ in. in diameter. A cut is made to the centre and the collar is put in place by overlapping and glueing the edges.

Next the face which is a flat shape (5) with eyes and mouth cut as indicated. It was an oval $2\frac{1}{2}$ in. wide by 3 in. long. This is glued in position to the top of the tube.

The hair is shape (6) curled and placed from the forehead over the back of the head. This was 7 in. long by $4\frac{1}{4}$ in. wide.

The hands are cut to shape as shown and glued in the sleeves.

Complete the figure (8) with the trumpet. This is an 8 in. cone of paper with the end made from a scored circle $2\frac{1}{2}$ in. in diameter (9).

NATIVITY SCENES

At Christmas, perhaps more than at any other time, decorations are required to decorate the home, churches, schools, etc. What better than scenes from the Nativity? These can be made in all white paper sculpture or they can be coloured with poster paints. Tradition credits St. Francis of Assisi with the introduction of figurines to show the Nativity at Christmastide. This custom is now practised all over the world. In Italy, south of France and central Europe, elaborate and beautiful Christmas cribs are featured with the Holy Family, the Shepherd, the Magi and animals arranged in a miniature panorama around the stable in Bethlehem. Illustrated are some of these figures made entirely of paper. They are quite simple to make as you will learn from the instructions given.

MAKING THE NATIVITY FIGURES

The six standing figures in the photographs were 10 in. in height and are all made from the same construction methods. The only variations giving them identity are the very simple additions of costume details, face details and hair styles.

CONSTRUCTION DETAILS FOR ONE OF THE THREE KINGS

These details given below also apply to the other five figures.

THE SUPPORT OR ARMATURE

This is made from a dowel of wood, 10 in. in height and $\frac{3}{8}$ in. in diameter which is glued to a circle of cardboard 4 in. in diameter. (See photo.)

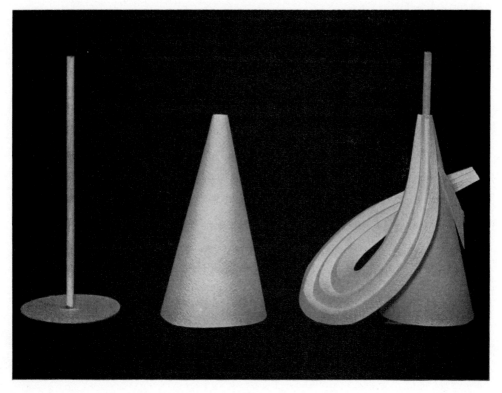

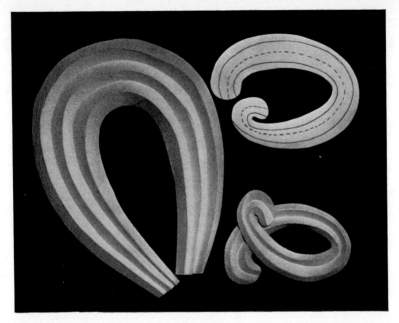

THE CONE BODY CONSTRUCTION

Each of the six figures, up to the neckline, is composed of a cone of paper, 8 in. in height and 4 in. in diameter at the base. The segments of paper used to make the cones are cut from a circle of paper 18 in. in diameter. Make up one of these cones and place it over the dowel support.

THE NECK AND HEAD PIECE

The neck and head is constructed upon a tube of paper, 3 in. square, rolled and glued into a tube $\frac{1}{2}$ in. in diameter. (See photo.) The face and head shape comes next. This is drawn and cut out of a piece of paper $3\frac{1}{2}$ in. long and $2\frac{1}{2}$ in. deep. This face and head shape will, of course, vary with each figure mainly at the chin. Having cut out the shape the face details can be painted in at this stage, or you may indicate the features with tiny pieces of paper glued in position upon the face. For a simple classical effect face details can be dispensed with especially if the design is to be left all white. In any case the face details should be kept as simple as possible. The face and head piece is now rolled around the neck tube fixing at an angle as shown with a spot of glue. (See photo.) Lay this completed head on one side and proceed.

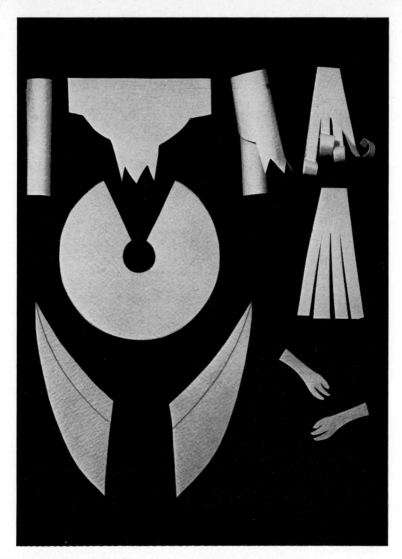

THE SLEEVES WHICH ALSO SERVE AS ARMS

The sleeves are drawn and cut out next. They are scored where indicated by the line, folded and then fixed in position to the top of the cone with a spot of glue on the pointed end only.

THE HANDS

The hands are drawn, cut out and fixed in position to the top of the sleeves with glue.

CLOAK FOR THE FIGURE OF THE KING

The cloak for this figure was made to the shape shown in the photograph by scoring reverse curves which were then folded into it. You have already been acquainted with these curves in the exercises. The completed cloak is now fixed in position to the shoulder at the top of the cone construction with glue. (See photo.)

The HEAD PIECE which you have already made is now placed over the dowel support after you have placed glue inside the tube neck construction at the back only. The tube should be pulled close to the top of the cone body. Trim a little if necessary here to allow the head to be level with the dowel top.

THE COLLAR WHICH ALSO INDICATES SHOULDER LINE

This is drawn with compasses on paper making a circle 4 in. in diameter, and another circle in the centre which is cut out. This is $\frac{3}{4}$ in. in diameter. Cut through to the centre as shown. (See photo.) This collar is now placed round the neck of the figure and pulled round into shape by overlapping the edges which should be previously glued.

THE HAIR STYLE

For this particular figure the hair was made from paper cut into strips and curled with the scissor blades as previously described in the exercises. These strips are then glued into the top of the head piece. The fringe is a piece of paper cut to shape, glued to the forehead, taken back over the top of the head and glued at the back.

THE CROWN AND GIFT PACKAGE

To complete this figure the crown is cut from a strip of paper and fixed around the head with a spot of glue. The gift package in this case was a tiny box of paper with a piece of paper curved over the top of it forming a curved lid to look like a gift casket.

COLOURING

Much pleasure can be had by colouring the figures with poster colours. These colours are recommended because they do not require the use of much moisture, and also glowing colours are obtainable. This particular figure was coloured as follows: the main cone body was

scarlet, cloak, collar and crown gold, hands and face light tan, beard, hair and face details black. The sleeves were white and the gift package gold. The colouring should be done after the pieces are made and before assembling them in position.

I also strongly advise that these figures should be made from good quality drawing paper of the hand-made variety.

KING TWO

Make up as previous figure. The cloak is just a segment of paper cut from a circle, rolled in at the front edges and glued around the figure. The head and neck piece to be made as previous figure but with a change of face details and with tiny ear-rings cut out and fixed to the head piece. After fixing the head piece make two collars, one 3 in. in diameter and the other 4 in. Cut and fit around the neckline. The hat is made from two circles of paper 2 in. in diameter with a 1 in. diameter circle scored into them. Cut to the centre of each and glue, overlapping the edges. Glue these pieces on top of each other in reverse to make the hat brim. The crown is a small cone of paper glued to this brim. The "gift" is fashioned from tubes of paper.

Colours: cone body and cone of hat—light green, face and hands—tan, the rest white.

KING THREE

Make up as previous figure. The cloak is a segment of paper cut from a circle, scored, pleated and fixed around the figure. Over this is a small draped collar. This is made as the draped cloak on a previous figure but smaller. The head and neck piece to be as the previous figure but with curled hair. The hat is a strip of paper placed around the head with a flat circle of paper for a top. Two circles are cut for collars, 3 and 4 in. in diameter. Cut, make and fix in position then cut them partly up the front. The gift package is a tiny box with paper trimming.

Colours: Cone body—light green, draped cloak, collar and hat—light green, the rest white.

MARY

Make up as previous figures. The face is a small oval shape fixed to a tube for the neck. The shoulder line collar is made up as previously and is $3\frac{1}{2}$ in. in diameter. Cut and fix around the neckline. The draped head-dress is made from the shape shown in the photograph scored into reverse curves and folded into shape. Place a strip of paper around the forehead and glue the draped head-dress over this at the top only. Allow to dry. Next bring the right side drape over the left and glue to the collar. Fix the other drape to the collar. (See finished model for this detail.) Finish the head-dress with a shaped piece of paper cut out and glued from the dowel at the top of the head and curving down the back of the figure.

Colours: Face and hands—flesh colour, cone body—celestial blue, the rest all white.

JOSEPH

This figure is made up as previous figures. A segment of paper again makes the short cloak. The head and face made as previously but in

this case the hair is a flat cut-out shape glued to the forehead and over to the back of the head. Two collars are made, 3 and 4 in. in diameter. Cut and place in position around the neck.

Colours: Body cone—blue, face and hands—tan, the rest yellow gold.

SHEPHERD

As previous figures except that the sleeves are made from small cones of paper placed under the cloak. The collars which finish the cloak are 2 and 3 in. in diameter. Cut and make up as for previous figures. The head-dress is a triangle of paper folded over to fit around the head. The shepherd's crook is cut from cardboard.

Colours: Body cone—scarlet, face and hands—tan, the rest white.

THE INFANT

This is just a simple shape, an oblong with a circle for a face cut from paper. Wrap the body with paper strips for clothes, the strips crossing over each other. The halo is a circle of paper scored with a smaller circle and fixed behind the head.

Colours: Face—flesh, halo—yellow gold, the rest white.

THE MANGER

Two X shaped pieces of cardboard between which a folded piece of cardboard is glued in position.

WHEN READING THESE INSTRUCTIONS FOR MAKING THE FIGURES IT IS IMPORTANT THAT YOU LOOK AT THE PHOTOGRAPHS OF THE FINISHED MODELS AS YOU PROCEED.

A CHRISTMAS REINDEER

Here is an interesting piece of paper sculpture which can be used in many ways—as a panel decoration in all white on a scarlet background, or it could be used for a Christmas card motif.

To make the reindeer—first draw and cut out in stout paper the whole animal. Next draw and cut out the paper overlay—making it a little larger than the original animal, score and fold where indicated by the plain and dotted lines and fix in position over the animal with spots of glue. Next the neck overlay is drawn, cut out and scored and folded, fix in position with glue. The ear is cut out and pulled into shape as you fix it in position with a spot of glue. The Holly is made as described in the section—making leaves.

The panel shown features two reindeers in reverse, the centre candle is a cardboard tube covered with paper, inside this glue a circle of card to take the paper flame. The background to the flame is made from pleated paper fixed with gum tape behind a circle of cardboard, which is glued behind the candle. The whole decoration is mounted upon a panel.